OMNIBUS EDITION

A New Tune A Day™
for Alto Saxophone
Books 1 & 2

The first 20 lessons of *A New Tune A Day* are designed to be used seamlessly with the clarinet edition.

Teachers wishing to accommodate both instruments in a lesson will be able to do so with almost every piece of every lesson, including the duets and rounds, except where indicated: *

look for this symbol within the book

The useful addition of chord symbols in the concert key for many of the pieces in this book will enable the teacher to provide an accompaniment on guitar or piano.

D0916174

Boston Music Company
part of The Music Sales Group
London/New York/Paris/Sydney/Copenhagen/Berlin/Madrid/Tokyo

Foreword

Since its appearance in the early 1930s, C. Paul Herfurth's original *A Tune A Day* series has become the most popular instrumental teaching method of all time. Countless music students have been set on their path by the clear, familiar, proven material, and the logical, sensibly-paced progression through the lessons within the book.

The teacher will find that the new books have been meticulously rewritten by experienced teachers: instrumental techniques and practices have been updated and the musical content has been completely overhauled.

The student will find clearly-presented, uncluttered material, with familiar tunes and a gentle introduction to the theoretical aspects of music. The books are now accompanied by audio CDs of examples and backing tracks to help the student develop a sense of rhythm, intonation and performance at an early stage.

As in the original books, tests are given following every five lessons. Teachers are encouraged to present these as an opportunity to ensure that the student has a good overview of the information studied up to this point.

The following extract from the foreword to the original edition remains as true today as the day it was written:

The value of learning to count aloud from the very beginning cannot be over-estimated. Only in this way can a pupil sense rhythm. Rhythm, one of the most essential elements of music, and usually conspicuous by its absence in amateur ensemble playing, is emphasized throughout.

Eventual success in mastering the instrument depends on regular and careful application to its technical demands. Daily practice should not extend beyond the limits of the player's physical endurance — the aim should be the gradual development of tone control alongside assured finger-work.

Music-making is a lifelong pleasure, and at its heart is a solid understanding of the principles of sound production and music theory. These books are designed to accompany the student on these crucial first steps: the rewards for study and practice are immediate and lasting.

Welcome to the world of music!

Published by
Boston Music Company

Exclusive Distributors:
Music Sales Corporation
257 Park Avenue South, New York, NY 10010, USA.
Music Sales Limited
14-15 Berners Street, London W1T 3LJ, England.
Music Sales Pty Limited
20 Resolution Drive, Caringbah, NSW 2229, Australia.

Your Guarantee of Quality
As publishers, we strive to produce every book to the highest commercial standards. The music has been freshly engraved and the book has been carefully designed to minimize awkward page turns and to make playing from it a real pleasure. Throughout, the printing and binding have been planned to ensure a sturdy, attractive publication which should give years of enjoyment. If your copy fails to meet our high standards, please inform us and we will gladly replace it.

Edited by David Harrison
Music processed by Paul Ewers Music Design
Original compositions and arrangements by Ned Bennett
Cover and book designed by Chloë Alexander
Photography by Matthew Ward
Models: Matthew Deacon and Fran Roper
Printed in the United States of America
  by Vicks Lithograph and Printing Corporation
Backing tracks by Guy Dagul
CD performance by Ned Bennett
CD recorded, mixed and mastered by Jonas Persson and John Rose

www.musicsales.com

Contents

Rudiments of music

The staff

Music is written on a grid of five lines called a *staff*.

At the beginning of each staff is placed a special symbol called a *clef* to describe the approximate range of the instrument for which the music is written.

This example shows a *treble clef*, generally used for melody instruments.

The staff is divided into equal sections of time, called *bars* or *measures*, by *barlines*.

Note values

Different symbols are used to show the time value of *notes*, and each *note value* has an equivalent symbol for a rest, representing silence.

The **eighth note**, often used to signify a half beat, is written with a solid head and a stem with a tail. The eighth-note rest is also shown.

The **quarter note**, often used to signify one beat, is written with a solid head and a stem. The quarter-note rest is also shown.

The **half note** is worth two quarter notes. It is written with a hollow head and a stem. The half-note rest is placed on the middle line.

The **whole note** is worth two half notes. It is written with a hollow head. The whole-note rest hangs from the fourth line.

Other note values

Note values can be increased by half by adding a dot after the note head. Here a half note and quarter note are together worth a *dotted* half note.

Grouping eighth notes

Where two or more eighth notes follow each other, they can be joined by a *beam* from stem to stem.

Time signatures

The number of beats in a bar is determined by the *time signature*, a pair of numbers placed after the clef.
The upper number shows how many beats each bar contains, while the lower number indicates what kind of note value
is used to represent a single beat. This lower number is a fraction of a whole note, so that 4 represents quarter notes
and 8 represents eighth notes.

C, for *common time*, is another way to write $\frac{4}{4}$.

6 means six eighth notes
8 to the bar.

4 means four quarter notes
4 to the bar.

3 means three quarter notes
4 to the bar.

Note names

Notes are named after the first seven letters of the alphabet and are written on lines or spaces on the staff,
according to pitch.

D E F G A B C D E F G

Accidentals

The pitch of a note can be altered up or down a half step (or *semitone*) by the use of sharp and flat symbols.
These temporary pitch changes are known as *accidentals*.

The *sharp* (♯) raises the pitch of a note.

The *natural* (♮) returns the note to its original pitch.

The *flat* (♭) lowers the pitch of a note.

Ledger lines

Ledger lines are used to extend the range of the staff for low or high notes.

C B A G A B C D

Barlines

Various different types of barlines are used:

Double barlines divide one section of music from another.

Final barlines show the end of a piece of music.

Repeat marks show a section to be repeated.

Before you play:

The saxophone and accessories

Your complete saxophone outfit should include the following:

• Saxophone main body

• Neck

• Reeds

• Sling

• Ligature

• Pull-through

A 30 A

ALTO Saxophone
+ BASS Clarinet
+ BASS Flute

• Mouthpiece cap

• Mouthpiece

Setting-up routine

1. Select a reed that is clean and undamaged (they are quite delicate); place the reed on your tongue, close your mouth and swirl saliva around the reed to moisten it.

It's important to make sure that the reed is good and moist before you begin to play.

2. While you are moistening the reed, push the neck fully into the top of the saxophone so that it extends in line with the thumb hook and rest. Tighten the key so the neck doesn't move. **Never pick the saxophone up by the neck**, just in case the key is not tightened as the body of the saxophone can fall off with disastrous results. Lay the saxophone aside carefully.

3. Attach the reed to the mouthpiece using the ligature. The end of the reed needs to be *exactly* level with and central to the tip of the mouthpiece. This can be a complicated operation at first.

The ligature should be tight enough to hold the reed firmly. When you've finished playing remove the reed and wipe off excess moisture before replacing it on the mouthpiece.

4. *Twist* the mouthpiece onto the cork at the end of the neck as far as it will comfortably go. Be careful not to dislodge the reed from its position. Make sure the mouthpiece is level when the saxophone is held vertically.

5. Place the sling around your neck, then attach the hook to the ring at the back of the saxophone.

Important *Always* use the pull-through to dry your saxophone after playing.

The exact position of the mouthpiece on the neck affects the tuning. Pull the mouthpiece off a little to lower the pitch, and push it on to raise it slightly — don't over-do it.

Spread a little grease on the cork from time to time to prevent cracking.

Lesson 1 goals:

1. **Breathing using the diaphragm**
2. **Posture and hand positioning**
3. **Formation of the mouth shape (embouchure)**
4. **Tonguing**
5. **The notes B, A and G**
6. **Counting while playing; whole notes, half notes, and quarter notes**

Breathing

A relaxed, controlled posture is essential for comfort and correct breathing.

When breathing in and out, always use your diaphragm. This is a large muscular membrane underneath your rib cage which causes your belly to go *out* when breathing in and to go *in* when breathing out.

You will be able to control your breathing far more effectively using your diaphragm than if you were to breathe with the *intercostal* muscles high up in your chest.

Exercise 1:

Breathe in counting four beats, then breathe out counting 4 and so on, always using the diaphragm and maintaining a steady flow of air.

In, 2, 3, 4,   Out, 2, 3, 4,   In...

Place one hand on your stomach to check whether it is going out as you breathe in then in when you breathe out.

Posture and holding the saxophone

Place the saxophone sling around your neck and attach the saxophone to the hook.

Stand in a relaxed, upright way, feet slightly apart.

Place your left thumb on the thumb button towards the top of the saxophone, and your right thumb underneath the curved support towards the bottom.

The fingers of each hand should curl around the body of the saxophone to the front, making sure they do not push against any keys at the sides.

Adjust the sling so that the mouthpiece enters your mouth without you having to crane your neck forwards or back.

Aim to keep a straight back and upright head when playing.

Embouchure

Say the letter *F* as in *foo* several times.
Notice how the top teeth push down on the
center of the bottom lip.

Rest your top teeth gently on the top of the
mouthpiece, about a centimeter or ⅜" from the tip.

Push your bottom lip upwards against the reed
without using your bottom teeth as support.

Now close the sides of your mouth around the
mouthpiece.

*The lips should
form a firm, airtight
seal around the
mouthpiece.
Make sure the cheeks
remain taught:
don't puff them out.*

Exercise 2:

Set your top teeth and bottom lip on the mouthpiece. Breathe in through the corners of your mouth over the
count of 4, close the mouth and breathe out attempting to produce a note. Don't puff out your cheeks.

- If you are able to play a note, well done – you are on your way!
- If you just hear the sound of air blowing down the saxophone, tighten your embouchure
  around the mouthpiece a bit, but don't bite.
- If the airway is blocked when you try to play, this is because you are closing the gap between
  the reed and the mouthpiece. Loosen your embouchure a bit.
- If you make a nasty squeak, it is probably because your bottom teeth are touching the reed.
  Remember it is the bottom lip that must support the reed.

Tonguing

Say the word *too* several times. The tongue acts as a valve that blocks the air until the precise moment that
the word is started. Notes on the saxophone should be started in this way to ensure a clean *attack*.

Breathe in and form the correct embouchure as described above. Place your tongue along the underside of
the reed so there is about a centimeter or ⅜" of contact, from the tip of the tongue to the tip of the reed.

Start a note by releasing the tongue from the reed as in the word *too*.
The note should have a definite and tidy beginning.

Exercise 3:

Play the following notes in time, ensuring you tongue each one.

Lesson 1

The notes B, A and G

Take a deep breath and then play the note, holding it for a few seconds.

	B
L1	●
L2	○ **left hand**
L3	○
R1	○
R2	○ **right hand**
R3	○

NOTE
The fingering diagrams throughout this book are shown from the player's point of view

Exercise 4:

Breathe before the beginning of this exercise and in the rests.

Don't forget to tongue each note. A four-beat note is called a **whole note**.

Exercise 5:

Each of the notes and rests here are **half notes,** worth two beats.

Exercise 6:

These notes and rests are all **quarter notes,** worth one beat each.

Breathe in quickly during quarter-note rests.

Pieces for Lesson 1

Valley Song

Going Cuckoo

Au Clair de la Lune

1. **The note C**
2. **Open-throat breathing**

3. **Dotted half notes**
4. **Three beats in a bar**

The note C

OPENING YOUR THROAT

Blow on the back of your hand. You will feel the air is cold. Now try again, pretending that you are steaming up a window. This time the air on the back of your hand should feel warm because you have just breathed out with your throat open. You should keep your throat open at all times when playing as it will improve your tone.

Exercise 1:

Stand with a relaxed posture, take a good deep breath and play the note with an open throat, using the diaphragm to control the air flow.

The symbol above this note is called a **pause**. It means you should hold the note for longer than its actual value of four beats. Hold this one for as long as you can. Play with an **open throat**.

Long notes like this one should be the first thing you practice every day.

Exercise 2:

Play these notes in tempo with an open throat. The little commas are *breath* marks.
Take a very quick breath here without disrupting the 4-beat count.

Exercise 3:

Changing fingers smoothly from C to B and back is very difficult. Play this exercise many times, starting slowly, then playing it more quickly as your coordination improves. Don't be satisfied with any untidiness!

Dotted notes

A dot placed to the right of a note multiplies its duration (value) by one and a half.

This means that a half note with a dot would increase in duration from two beats to three (2+1=3).

Count: 1   2   3   4   1   2   3   4

Exercise 4:

Count carefully as you play these notes. Remember the open throat.

Time signatures

So far all the exercises and pieces have had a **time signature** of four beats to every bar:

1, 2, 3, 4, **1**, 2, 3, 4, **1**, 2, 3, 4 etc.

Many pieces, however, contain three beats per bar.

This means that the count in your head will be **1**, 2, 3, **1**, 2, 3, **1**, 2, 3 etc.

A waltz is a dance that uses this time signature.

Exercise 5:

Count three beats per bar, as shown by the top number of the time signature, and make sure you don't get confused between notes in spaces (A and C) and notes on lines (G and B).

Count: 1 2 3   1 2 3   1 2 3

THINK!
Are you still relaxed when you play? Remember to keep your shoulders down and breathe using your diaphragm.

Check that your bottom lip is not being drawn inwards when you play: the support for the reed needs to be in the lip, not the bottom teeth.

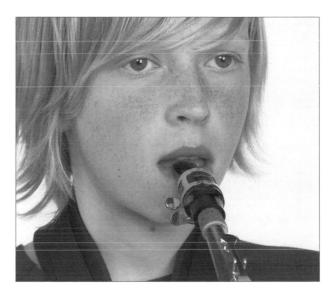

Check the lip: the support for the reed needs to be in the lip, not the bottom teeth.

13

Pieces for Lesson 2

Back To Bed

Grumpy Graham

Medieval Dance

Barcarolle

Offenbach

goals:

1. **The octave key**
2. **The note D with the octave key**
3. **Tied notes**

The octave key

You will probably have noticed the only key on the back of the saxophone. This is the octave key and is operated by your left thumb. The thumb must roll upwards onto this key and not be lifted from the thumb rest. You will need to press this key to play all notes above the D that you will learn in this lesson. When you play notes which require the octave key, a little extra air support from the diaphragm will be required, and be careful not to squeeze the reed.

The octave key is used for all notes from this D up. Let the thumb sit on the thumb rest in such a way that you can comfortably press the key down when needed.

The note D

You need three fingers in each hand for this note, as well as the octave key.

Remember to stand comfortably with relaxed shoulders. The modern saxophone is designed so that you shouldn't have to stretch to reach the keys, however make sure you are not pushing any of the keys at the sides of the instrument.

Breathe with the diaphragm and with an open throat. Increase the support in your bottom lip a little.

Exercise 1:

Play this one a few times, holding the note for as long as is comfortable.

Exercise 2:

Remember to tongue the beginning of each note.

Exercise 3:

Play this one many times to ensure that your tongue, fingers and thumb (if needed) all move together.

Exercise 4:

Don't get confused between G, B and D, which all look a bit similar.

Ties and tied notes

Two notes of the same pitch can be joined together to make a longer note by *tying* them together. A curved line is drawn from one to the other to show this. The note is then held on for the *combined value* of the two notes. This is usually needed if a note needs to carry on into the next bar.

Here are some examples:

is held for **3** beats   is held for **6** beats

Exercise 5:

Count very carefully here.

Count: 1   2   3   4   1   2...

THINK!

Are you playing with *warm air* because your throat is open?

Is your thumb rolling to push the octave key, not lifting?

Pieces for Lesson 3

Jingle Bells

CD1 12–13

Largo (from the New World Symphony)

Dvořák

CD1 14–15

Lightly Row

CD1 16

Student

Teacher

Knight Time

CD1 17–18

goals:

1. The note E with the octave key
2. Dynamics (loud and soft)
3. Slurred notes

E

The note E

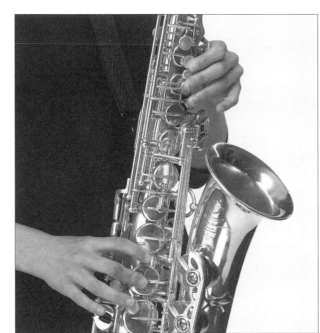

Remember to roll your thumb to the octave key, and to use your diaphragm to provide a little extra air for these higher notes.

Exercise 1:

Rolling the octave key.

Dynamics

Notes and rhythms are two of the elements of music, but without expression, music can be lifeless and mechanical. One of the obvious ways of introducing *color* into music is to play sections of pieces or phrases at different levels of loudness.

f stands for the word *forte* and means loud.   *p* stands for the word *piano* which means quiet.

Exercise 2:

Play these notes according to the dynamic displayed underneath.

Use your diaphragm to increase the air flow for the loud notes, and decrease the air flow for the quiet ones.

It's often harder to play a piece slowly and accurately than to bluff your way through it quickly.

Take your time and aim for a clear, confident style.

Exercise 3:

This is a note-twister. Try it slowly at first, then try to build up speed each time you practice it.

Can you play it in one breath?

Exercise 4:

These notes are all written on spaces. Don't get A, C and E confused.

Slurs

In all the pieces and exercises so far you have tongued every note; that is, you have started each note with a *T* as in *too*. This can make the music sound a bit disjointed, and spoils the flow of gentle pieces such as *Barcarolle* in lesson 2.

Music is made smoother by slurring notes together. This means you should only tongue the note where the slur begins. All other notes included in the slur are played by just changing the fingering.
Slurs are shown by lines which look like ties, but the notes will be of different pitches.

Be sure to give a clean, crisp end to your notes by bringing your tongue back onto the reed rather than by just stopping breathing, especially at the end of a piece or at a rest.

Exercise 5: slurred pairs

Only tongue the first of each pair of notes, but keep the air flowing as you play the second.

Exercise 6:

Here you need to slur three notes at a time. The steady 1, 2, 3 count is unaffected by slurs.

Exercise 7:

Try *Barcarolle* again with slurs and with the dynamic shown. It should sound much more like a lullaby.

Pieces for Lesson 4

CD1 19–20

When The Saints Go Marching In

CD1 21–22

Joshua Fought The Battle Of Jericho

Spiritual

CD1 23–24

Coventry Carol (adapted)

Canon For Two

The second player begins one bar behind the first player.

goals:

1. **The note C sharp (C♯)**
2. **Tones and Semitones**
3. **Repeat signs**

The note C♯

As no fingers are required for this note, extra care must be taken to keep the saxophone from moving around. Keep your fingers curled over the front keys, but don't close any of them.

Compare this note with C and D.
You will hear that C♯ is halfway between.

The difference in pitch between C and D is called a **tone**.
C to C♯ is only a **semitone**.
C♯ to D is also a **semitone**.

A semitone is the smallest *interval* that can be played on most instruments.

Exercise 1:
Get used to holding the saxophone when playing C♯.

Exercise 2:
Compare C to D (a tone) with C to C♯ (a semitone). The *natural* sign is to remind you when to play a normal C.

The thick barlines with two dots tell you to **repeat** the music between them—in other words, play twice.

Repeat sign

Exercise 3: sharps and naturals
All the Cs here are natural unless they have a sharp symbol immediately before them or they come after a C♯ in the same bar and don't have a natural sign.

Pieces for Lesson 5

CD1 25–26

Jingle Bells

CD1 27

Abide With Me

Monk

CD1 28–29

Juggling

test: *for* Lessons 1 to 5

1. Note duration

On the staff below, draw notes of the indicated duration:

(4)

2. Rests

On the staff below, draw rests of the indicated duration:

(4)

3. Notes

On the staff below, draw the following notes as half notes:

G, B, E, C, A, D and **C♯**

(8)

4. Sharp thinking

How many **C♯**s do you play in this piece? _____

(2)

5. Bars

Draw barlines on this staff where they are needed.

(7)

Total **(25)**

Lesson 6 goals:

1. **The note F sharp (F♯)**
2. **Key signatures and their meaning**
3. **The keys of C, G and D majors**

The note F♯

This note is a semitone below G.

Exercise 1:

Listen to how close F♯ and G sound.

Exercise 2: wide leaps

Although the notes are a long way from each other, only a few fingers have to move. Play this as cleanly as you can.

Different keys

If you try to sing a simple tune such as *The Star Spangled Banner*, you may find early on that you can't reach the high notes without really straining. The solution is to start the piece a little lower. This time, you may be able to sing the high notes perfectly. You are now singing the piece in a different key.

There are many different keys in music, each of which needs its own set of notes. The key of **C major** is easy as it requires no sharps. The key of **G major** requires all **F**s to be played as **F♯**. The key of **D** requires all **F**s and **C**s to be played as **F♯** and **C♯**. These necessary alterations will be shown as the **key signature** at the beginning of every line of music.

Exercise 3: comparison

Play the opening to this well-known carol first in the key of C major, then in the key of D major.
Notice that the key signature tells you that all Cs are in fact C♯s, otherwise the tune will sound wrong.

Pieces for Lesson 6

Barcarolle

(Learn the bottom part this time!)

Offenbach

CD1 11

In Paris

CD1 30 31

> ## THINK!
>
> Do you start every practice session with long notes? They are the best way to improve your tone and build up your strength.

Pieces for Lesson 6

When The Saints Go Marching In

The key of this piece is A major, but don't worry about the G♯ in the key signature...
you won't need to play a G♯.

Steal Away

Spiritual

From *The Unfinished Symphony*

Schubert

Count up to 6 in each bar for this one, and watch out for the C♯s!

Pieces for Lesson 6

Nkosi Sikelel'

E. Mankayi Sontonga

CD1 38

Magnetic Forks

CD1 39

Lesson 7

goals:

1. **The notes E and D**
2. **Octaves**
3. **Common time**

The notes E and D

E

D

Octaves

Practice makes perfect. Perseverance will be rewarded with a good, strong tone.

Make sure you are breathing from your diaphragm for complete breath control, and experiment with your embouchure. And most important of all: relax!

You have already seen how to play the notes D and E in lessons 3 and 4. However, the new notes for this lesson are played without the octave key: they sound the same but rather lower.

Exercise 1:

Compare the sounds of low E with the *higher* E and low D with the *higher* D.

The large $\mathbf{C}$ at the beginning of this staff is shorthand for **common time,** which is the same as $\frac{4}{4}$.

Exercise 2:

Low notes can be hard to play. Ensure that your throat is open. Imagine trying to steam up the inside of the saxophone with your breath.

Pieces for Lesson 7

O Come All Ye Faithful

Skye Boat Song

Scottish traditional

Repeat the section within the repeat signs, then go back to the beginning and play until
the sign *Fine* (Italian for "end").

Scarborough Fair

English traditional

You could play the top part or the bottom part. If you feel ambitious, learn both!

Lesson 8 goals:

1. **Eighth notes**
2. **D major scale**
3. **Tempo and character markings**

Eighth notes

Sight-reading (playing music that you haven't seen before) is an important skill for a musician.

Get into the habit of finding music you haven't played before and trying to play it straight off. You'll be surprised how much easier this becomes once you get used to it.

Remember to keep a steady beat and the rhythm will take care of itself.

So far you have studied and played notes that last for four beats (whole note), two beats (half note), and one beat (quarter note). You have also learned how to increase note durations by tying notes together or by adding a dot to a half note (for a three-beat note).

Eighth note are notes which last for *half* the length of a quarter note and should therefore be played *twice* as fast.

Single eighths and an eighth rest

Eighths in pairs (worth 1 quarter per pair)

Eighths as a group (a half-note's worth)

Exercise 1: *double or quit!*

Keep the beat steady and don't start too quickly.

Count: 1 2 3 4   1 2 3 4   1 2 3 4   1 & 2 & 3 & 4 &   1 2 3 4

Exercise 2: three beats per bar

Count: 1 2 3   1 2 3   1 & 2 & 3 &   1 2 3

Exercise 3: the scale of D major

Play your scales steadily and slowly – try to make the notes sound as though they belong together.

A scale is a series of notes that move up or down by step from one note to the same note an octave higher or lower. Play this both slurred and tongued (as shown by the dotted slur lines).

Pieces for Lesson 8

Some short melodies for practice at playing eighth notes.

Yankee Doodle

This piece has only two beats per bar, and notice the tempo (speed) marking above the beginning of the piece.

Can Can

Offenbach

Nessun Dorma

Puccini

From *The Magic Flute*

Mozart

Swing Low, Sweet Chariot

Spiritual

goals:

1. **The notes low and high F**
2. **Dotted quarter notes**
3. **Anacrusis (upbeat)**

The notes low and high F

Exercise 1:

Play each note for as long as you can. Every time you practice you should start with long notes!

Dotted quarter notes

Dotted notes are often used instead of tying notes together: the fewer symbols there are on the page, the easier the music is to read.

As long ago as lesson 2 you discovered that a dot placed to the right of a half note increased its value from two beats to three. You could say that the dot *multiplies* its length by one and a half.

The same dot can be used to increase a quarter note's length from one beat to one and a half beats. In other words, instead of being the same length as two eighths tied together, its value is raised to three eighths.

Exercise 2:

Play this slowly so that you can count each eighth note. Learn to recognize the rhythms as you recognize words without really having to read them.

Count: 1 & 2 & 3 & 4 & 1 & 2 & 3 & 4 & 1...

Exercise 3:

Play this exercise a few times increasing the speed a little each time. In time you should feel the rhythm by recognizing the pattern of notes and rely less on having to count each eighth note.

Exercise 4:

Because this type of rhythm is very common but a little tricky, here is another exercise.

This time there are three beats to a bar.

Anacrusis

Sometimes a piece of music doesn't begin with a whole bar.

The next piece begins with a single beat representing the last beat of a bar. This short bar (called an *upbeat* or *anacrusis*) is balanced by another short bar at the end. The two short bars add up to a whole bar.

Pieces for Lesson 9

Auld Lang Syne

Pieces for Lesson 9

Allegro from *Spring* (adapted)

Vivaldi

Allegro is the Italian word for quick and is very commonly seen as a tempo marking in music.
The top line here is the main tune, but you could also learn the bottom line for duet playing.

> ### THINK!
> Are you practicing properly?
> Always start with long notes, making sure you are using your diaphragm
> and open throat. Practice your exercises every day to build up that bottom lip
> strength and don't be satisfied if a piece is nearly right.
> It needs to be completely right before you should move on.

goals:

1. **The note low C**
2. **More dynamics**

The note low C

As with the other low notes (E and D) you must ensure that you play this note with an open throat. It is fun to make this note sound like a fog horn, but remember that if you can control your breathing the note will sound just as musical as all the others.

Exercise 1:

Play these long notes with an open throat and controlled breath.

Exercise 2:

Here is a *scale* of C major. Practice this first with every note tongued, then with all slurred. You will need to take a big breath.

More dynamics

Only *p* and *f* have been introduced so far. These tell you to play either quietly or loudly, however, in between these extremes you could play *moderately quiet* or *moderately loud*.
These are shown by the markings *mp* and *mf*. The *m* is short for *mezzo* which is the Italian word for half.

Try to make sure that the first forte is exactly as loud as the second forte: it's easy to lose track of just how loud you are, especially when the dynamics vary so much.

*Watch out that your **mp** isn't too quiet, otherwise you won't be able to come down further for the **p**.*

Exercise 3:

Play these notes with the dynamics indicated.

Pieces for Lesson 10

Silent Night

Gruber

Watch out for the low C at the end. Don't wake everybody up!

CD1
60–61

Dixie

Emmett

CD1
62

From *Symphony No.9* (play either part)

Beethoven

test: *for* Lessons 6 to 10

1. Note duration

On the staff below, draw notes of the indicated duration:

| 1 eighth note | 2 beats' worth of eighth notes | dotted quarter note | a note that lasts for 5 eighth notes |

(8)

2. Scale

On the staff below, draw the D major scale including the correct key signature:

(4)

3. Notes

On the staff below draw the following notes as quarter notes:

C, low C, high E, F♯, low D, high F, B, C♯

(4)

4. Dynamics

What are the Italian words for:

Moderately loud _____

Moderately quiet _____

(4)

5. Naming ceremony

Identify all the items indicated by arrows.

(5)

Total **(25)**

goals:

1. **The note B flat (B♭)**
2. **The key of F major**

The note B♭

The **flat** symbol *lowers* the note to which it applies by one semitone. This means that B♭ is a semitone below B, and a semitone above A.

Exercise 1:

Keep covering the keys at the front of your right hand when pushing the side key with the top of your palm.

B♭

Exercise 2:

The key signature of F major is one flat: B♭. Practice this scale both tongued and slurred.

There is an alternative fingering (see left) for the note B♭ that conveniently uses just one finger, which covers the *bis* key as well as the normal B.

This may feel strange at first, but you should get used to it as soon as possible. Try exercises 1 and 2 with this fingering instead.

In general, use the bis key for all B♭s unless there is a B natural (B♮) just before it or just after it.

Exercise 3:

Side B♭ or bis B♭?

B♭

Pieces for Lesson 11

Frère Jacques

French traditional

Up to four people can play this as a round. Begin when the previous instrument reaches the star in the third bar. Use the bis key for B♭ at all times here.

Romance No.1

Beethoven

CD1
63-64

Both fingerings for B♭ are needed in this piece.

Can Can

Offenbach

CD1
65-66

Compare this version in F major with the one in D major in lesson 8.

goals:

1. **The notes G, A, B, and C with the octave key**

2. **The note high D**
3. *D.S. al Fine*

The notes G, A, B, and C with the octave key

You might find that these high notes sound a little out of tune when you first play them.

Keep a firm embouchure to ensure a steady tone and correct tuning.

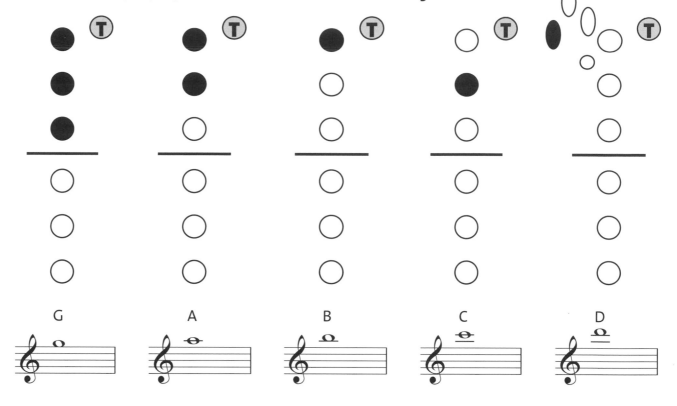

Exercise 1:

There are some wide leaps in this exercise. Remember to keep the tone even.

Exercise 2:

Make sure these octave leaps remain in tune as you go up.

Exercise 3:

Recognizing higher notes.

Pieces for Lesson 12

When The Saints Go Marching In

Play the section between the repeat bars twice. The first time, play the two bars at the end labeled 1, the second time play the bars labeled 2. These are called *first and second time endings*.

Reveille

Military traditional

D.S. al Fine means go back to the sign (𝄋) and play again until *Fine* (end).

Lesson 13 goals:

1. **The note F# with the octave key**
2. **Finger dexterity**

The note F# with the octave key

Fast fingers

This is the *"don't run before you can walk"* bit.

In order to play fast pieces, you must first spend time playing exercises and pieces slowly in order to gain complete control over every muscle that is being used.

Exercise 1:

This may seem easy, but aim for a perfect tone and precise finger movement.

Exercise 2:

Coordinating your right-hand fingers to play F to F# can be hard. Be really critical of yourself: if it's not entirely perfect more practice is needed.

Exercise 3:

Play this many times to build up speed.

Practice will help to build up "muscle memory": eventually you won't have to think about which fingers are required for a particular note, as your hands will "know" what to do.

Exercise 4:

Build up speed until you can play this really quickly.

Exercise 5: scales of G and C major

Every aspect of this must be perfect.

Pieces for Lesson 13

Camptown Races

Foster

Home On The Range

Pieces for Lesson 13

Danny Boy

Irish traditional

This is one of the most beautiful tunes ever written. Spend time on this to ensure complete fluency, control of dynamics and the correct slurs – it will be time well spent.

Swing Low, Sweet Chariot

Spiritual

goals:

1. **The note G sharp (G♯)**
2. **Minor keys and scales**

The note G♯

G♯

G♯ + octave key

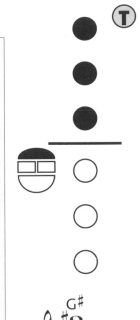

G♯

Exercise 1: low G, G♯ and A

This really works your little finger!

Try playing in front of the mirror to keep an eye on which key your left hand little finger should be playing. Eventually the placement of fingers will come naturally.

Exercise 2:

The more you practice the G♯, the stronger your little finger will become, so here goes:

Exercise 3:

The following piece does not appear in the Clarinet book *

A finger-twisting Scottish tune.

Lesson 14

Major and Minor

Most of the pieces you have played up to now have sounded cheerful. That is because they are virtually all in a *major* key, C major, F major, G major and so on. Sometimes, however, a composer wishes to express sadness in a piece. In general he or she will do this by writing the piece in a *minor* key.

Some people think of major keys as being bright, while minor keys are dark.

The mood created has to do with the sequence of intervals that makes up the scale for the key.

Exercise 4: the A major scale

Play this a few times and listen to its bright character.

Exercise 5: A minor

The *key signature* is the same as C major, however look out for the G♯s which are shown as they occur in the music. (These are called **accidentals**.)

Pieces for Lesson 14

Hava Nagila

Israeli traditional

A famous tune in a minor key (Dm). Start slowly and get faster as you go along.

This should sound very exciting!

46

Pieces for Lesson 14

Go Down Moses

Spiritual

The melody is divided up among the three saxophones so they are all equally important.

Use the written dynamics to blend in when you are playing an accompanying line.

Slowly

Lesson 15 goals:

1. **The notes C# and E with the octave key**
2. **Staccato and legato**

The note C#

C#

E + octave key

E

Exercise 1:

High notes only use a very short length of the instrument to make a sound. For this reason they need less breath for the same volume than a low note. Be careful not to use too much breath on high notes, otherwise it may affect the tone and the tuning — and your ears!

Remember diaphragm support for high notes and don't tighten the embouchure.

Keep your fingers close to the sax.

Exercise 2:

This is an E minor arpeggio extending over two octaves.

Exercise 3: low and high

Play slowly to ensure a warm and even tone for all notes.

Staccato and legato

Legato means "joined up" and refers to notes that are slurred or tongued smoothly without a gap from the previous one. *Staccato*, on the other hand, means "detached." This is shown by a dot above or below the note.

Exercise 4:

Repeat this many times to achieve clear staccato tonguing.

Exercise 5:

Begin this very slowly otherwise the eighth notes will be too fast to tongue.

Pieces for Lesson 15

The Blue Danube Waltz

Johann Strauss II

Steadily

Pieces for Lesson 15

CD1 78–79

Oh! Susannah

Stephen Foster

Quickly

CD1 80–81

Song Of The Volga Boatmen

Russian traditional

Gravely

CD1 82–83

Mango Walk

Jamaican traditional

Moderately

1. Key signatures

On the staff below, draw the correct key signatures for:

G major F major A minor A major C major

(5)

2. Dots

Simplify the music on the left using dots to get rid of the ties.

(5)

3. Notes

On the staff below draw the following notes as quarter notes:

G♯, low C, high D, B♭, F♯, high E

(6)

4. Articulation

What do the following words mean?

legato _____

staccato _____

(4)

5. Naming ceremony

Identify all the items indicated by arrows.

(5)

Total (25)

goals:

1. **The notes E flat (E♭) and B♭ with the octave key**
2. **Enharmonic notes**

The notes E♭ and B♭ with the octave key

Compare the three E♭ notes in different octaves.

Try to keep the tone as similar as possible despite the big difference in pitch. They should all sound as though they are coming from the same instrument.

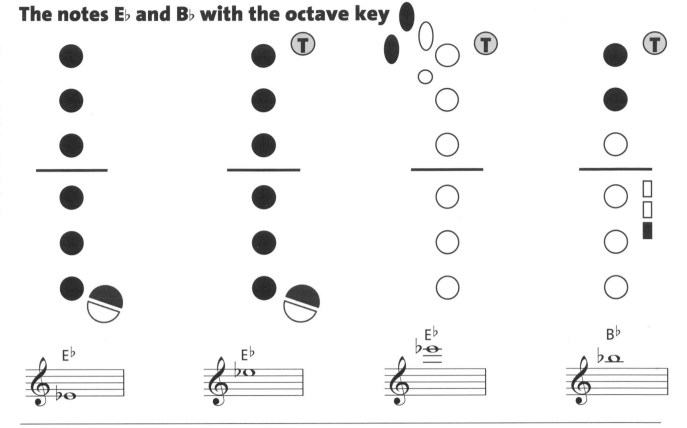

Exercise 1:

Play these long notes. Use a full breath for each one.

Enharmonic notes

From previous lessons, you will know that E♭ is a semitone *below* E, and at the same time a semitone *above* D. This means that the same note could be called D♯. These two notes are *enharmonic equivalents*.

Exercise 2:

These two short pieces need a note you have just learned, the first as a D♯, the second as an E♭.

Exercise 2:

Play the following notes. You *do* know the fingering for each one, however you may need to write down their enharmonic equivalents first.

Pieces for Lesson 16

The Entertainer

Scott Joplin

CD1 **84**

Enharmonic Blues

CD1 **85–86**

Lesson 17 goals:

1. **Gradation of dynamics**
2. **More Italian terms**

Dynamic markings and tempo markings are very useful.

Music should always be expressive, and these markings will give a clue to the way a piece should be played.

All dynamic changes you have played so far have been instant. However, suddenly changing from *piano* to *forte* has a different impact from a gradual change.

Crescendo means gradually get louder,

also shown as: ◁═════

Diminuendo means gradually get quieter,

also shown as: ═════▷

Some other commonly used Italian words to describe a tempo are:

Allegro quickly

Andante at a walking pace

Adagio slowly

Rallentando (rall.) becoming slower

Accelerando (accel.) becoming faster

Pieces for Lesson 17

La Forza del Destino

Verdi

Hail The Conquering Hero (from *Judas Maccabeus*)

Handel

William Tell Overture

Rossini

Lesson 18 goals:

1. **Swing eighths**
2. **Playing jazz pieces**

Swing

Remember not to play the eighths too "straight," but instead give them a healthy bounce.

You might imagine the beat divided into three, with the first two-thirds for the first eighth and the final third for the second eighth.

In classical music all eighth notes are played exactly as written, that is, lasting half as long as a quarter note.

In jazz, however, eighth notes are normally played unevenly, with the first of each pair longer than half a beat, and the second shorter to compensate. This is called **swing.**

Exercise 1:

Play this E minor scale in swing rhythm. Try it first all tongued, then with the slurs as written.

Pieces for Lesson 18

CD1 90–91

Little Brown Jug

CD1 92–93

Joshua Jazz

Pieces for Lesson 18

Maryland, My Maryland

Lesson 19 goals:

1. **Good technique through scale practice**
2. **Ensemble playing**

Practicing

Practicing scales every day will help you to:

- Train your fingers to respond quickly in various keys
- Ensure evenness in the timing of notes
- Develop a consistent tone over the instrument's range
- Increase control over your breathing
- Improve your listening awareness of note relationships

The following scales and arpeggios are recommended practice for saxophonists at a relatively early stage. They should be practiced both slurred and tongued.

F major

G major

D major (2 octaves)

D minor

A minor

58

Pieces for Lesson 19

Gypsy Rover

Pieces for Lesson 19

Down By The Riverside

Lively swing

goals:

1. $\frac{6}{8}$ time signature (compound time)
2. Traditional-style songs in $\frac{6}{8}$ time

Simple and compound time

$\frac{2}{4}$, $\frac{3}{4}$, and $\frac{4}{4}$ are all *simple* time signatures.

The top number tells you how many beats per bar, and the bottom number tells you that each beat is worth one quarter note. This also means that each beat can be divided into **two** eighth notes.

Exercise 1: counting in simple time

Count: 1   2   3   4   1 & 2 & 3 & 4 & 1...

In *compound* time, however, each beat is worth **three** eighth notes.

This means that each beat must now be a *dotted* quarter note.

Exercise 2: counting in compound time

Count: 1   &   a   2   &   a   1   &   a   2   &   a   1   2

Exercise 3:

Here's a well-known tune in $\frac{6}{8}$ time. Remember to think in *two*.

Count: 1 & a 2 & a   1 & a 2 & a   1 & a 2 & a   1 etc...

Irish jigs are in $\frac{6}{8}$ time, as is the well-known "We're Off To See The Wizard" from The Wizard Of Oz. $\frac{6}{8}$ pieces are often lively. Counting two groups of three is much easier than trying to count all six eighth notes.

T H I N K !

Remember to keep a steady beat. You might want to use a metronome. Some people like to tap their foot when they play, but this takes a little practice before it comes naturally.

Pieces for Lesson 20

The Animals Went In Two By Two

Traditional

For He's A Jolly Good Fellow

Traditional

1. Enharmonic

Rewrite the following notes as their enharmonic equivalents:

(5)

2. Afraid of heights?

Write the following music one octave higher:

(6)

3. Breath control

Play this note with a steady tone, controlling your breath at all times.

You will score one point (up to a maximum of five) for every three seconds held.

(5)

4. Expression

Write the Italian words for:

Get louder _____   Get quieter _____

Get quicker _____   Get slower _____

(4)

5. Scale test

Play the following from memory:

1. **D minor scale**

2. **D major arpeggio**

3. **F major scale**

4. **G major arpeggio**

5. **A minor scale**

(5)

Total (25)

goals:

1. The note low C♯
2. Sixteenth notes

The note low C♯

C♯

Exercise 1:

Long low notes are essential for improving your tone.

Breathe in over three seconds and play each note for between five and ten seconds.

Sixteenth notes

You should already be familiar with notes that last four beats (whole note), two beats (half note), one beat (quarter note), and half a beat (eighth note).

Sixteenth notes last for a *quarter* of the length of a quarter note, or *half* the length of an eighth note.

Single sixteenth note and a sixteenth-note rest

Group of four sixteenth notes (worth one quarter note)

One bar of sixteenth notes in 4/4 time

Exercise 2: Double Or Nothing!

Keep the beat steady and don't start too quickly.

Count: 1 2 3 4   1 2 3 4   1 2 3 4   1   2   3   4   1   2   3   4   1 2 3 4

Exercise 3: Three beats per bar

Pieces for Lesson 21

Ballad

Ned Bennett

A ballad is a slow jazz piece. Don't *swing* the eighth notes.

Surprise Symphony (excerpt)

Haydn

The surprise is in the 8th bar of this famous piece. Legend has it that the composer knew that his employer, Count Esterházy, often fell asleep during concerts. The sudden loud note was to wake him up!

Pieces for Lesson 21

CD2
5–6

Dracula's Dance

Ned Bennett

Sixteenth notes can look scary at first. Practice this very slowly making sure that your half notes, quarter notes, eighth notes, and sixteenth notes are played in tempo.

goals:

1. **The notes low B and low B flat (B♭)**
2. **Sixteenth-note groups**

The note low B

The note low B♭

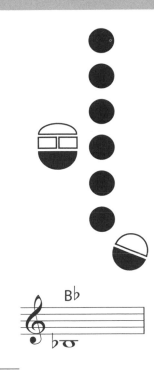

Exercise 1:

You will be practicing strength and positions of your little finger, and low notes which require an open throat.

Try to control the volume in this exercise otherwise the neighbors may complain!

In the exercises and pieces of the previous lesson, all the sixteenth notes were in groups of four lasting one beat in total. Below are three commonly seen combinations of eighth notes and sixteenth notes, all grouped together to make up one beat's worth of notes.

Try to learn these patterns as rhythmic words rather than trying to count them each time.

Exercise 2:

Exercise 3:

Exercise 4:

Pieces for Lesson 22

CD2 7

Simple Gifts

Joseph Bracket, Jr.

CD2 8-9

Frith Street Rag

Ned Bennett

Remember to read the grouped notes as *rhythmic words*.

Moderately

Pieces for Lesson 22

Dance Of The Swans

Tchaikovsky

TEMPO TERMS

There are a number of articulation markings in this piece including staccato, tenuto, and accent markings.

They occur early in the piece, but you must apply the same articulation later on, even if none is marked, in order to achieve a consistent performance.

Allegretto means "a little *Allegro*," being somewhere between **Andante** and **Allegro** in tempo.

Dotted pairs

The "dotted pair" is a very common rhythm: a dotted eighth note (worth three sixteenth notes) followed by a sixteenth note. Look at these three examples:

The first note of each pair is three times longer than the second. In the final example, the dotted eighth note is worth 3 sixteenth notes. The final sixteenth note completes the group (worth one quarter note in total).

Exercise 1:

It is very important to keep the 3:1 ratio between the dotted pairs, otherwise they could sound like swing eighth notes which are played in a more relaxed way (more like 2:1).

Exercise 2:

Try playing this entire exercise in tempo. Professional musicians often practice scales in this rhythm as it helps develop coordination between the tongue and the fingers.

The Scotch snap

The Scotch snap is the opposite of the dotted pair.
The sixteenth note comes first, then the dotted eighth note:

Exercise 3:

Here is a note pattern based on the F major scale using dotted pairs and Scotch snaps. Listen to how this sounds, then try to repeat this exercise in the keys of G, D, and C major.

Pieces for Lesson 23

Prelude

Chopin

Loch Lomond

Scottish Traditional

Watch out for the Scotch snap rhythms in this one!

Humoresque

Dvořák

The dotted pairs here are grouped to show each half bar or half note's-worth.

Make sure you don't swing this piece. Keep the dotted pairs light and accurate.

goals:

1. **Playing in tune**
2. **Sixteenth notes in 6/8**

Playing in tune

Expert musicians, no matter what instrument they play, are ones who are fussy about the details relating to their instrument. Here, you are going to focus on one vital detail of saxophone playing.

No saxophone, however expensive, will automatically play in tune. Professional saxophonists make very small adjustments to their embouchure to lower or raise notes by minuscule amounts. These adjustments must become second nature, otherwise there is too much to think about when you are playing a piece.

Exercise 1:

Make sure you have *warmed up* your saxophone.

Play a long F♯ with your correct embouchure (this will be the note A on the piano). Make sure you are perfectly in tune with the piano or CD tuning note. If you are sharp (too high), twist your mouthpiece out a little.

Do the opposite if you are flat (too low).
Your teacher will be able to guide you.

CD2 16

Now play the following music (in tempo) along with the CD or piano, listening very carefully to every note.

If you are in tune, the note will sound pure. If you are sharp, there will be an uncomfortable, grating sound. You will find that you may have to lower the higher notes by dropping your lower jaw a fraction. In this case, apply a little more pressure from your diaphragm to ensure a solid tone.

Intonation is the word for tuning individual notes. Good intonation takes a while to achieve.
Play this exercise at least three times a week.

Lesson 24

Sixteenth notes in 6/8 time

Below are pairs of sixteenth notes within half a 6/8 bar. As you did with the simple time groups, try to learn these rhythms as words. They have been labeled A to J.

A   B   C

The following groups contain 4 or 6 sixteenth notes:

D   E   F

And of course dotted pairs may also occur in 6/8:

G   H   I   J

Exercise 2: Combining the groups

Choose a series of 8 groups at random and write it down. Then clap the rhythm that the groups produce.
As each group contains three eighth notes' worth of beats, your piece will be four bars long in 6/8.
Here is an example:

B   D   H   A   I   D   F   G

Pieces for Lesson 24

CD2 17

Greensleeves

Attrib. Henry VIII

A well-known melody for practice at playing dotted pairs in 6/8 time. Are you playing the high notes in tune?

Pieces for Lesson 24

Lillabullero

17th Century

Allegro Moderato

Justano Bardi

goals:

1. **The chromatic scale**
2. **Good intonation through duet playing**

The chromatic scale

Chromatic literally means "colored." The chromatic scale is colored by every note that can be played on your instrument. Each note is one semitone above or below the last one.

Exercise 1:

Play one octave of the chromatic scale starting on G, ascending and descending.

You will find it is best to use the side B♭ fingering when needed.

Exercise 2:

Now play the chromatic scale starting on E.

Did you notice that this uses exactly the same notes?

You can start and finish the chromatic scale wherever you like, but the notes will always be the same.

Exercise 3:

A chromatic exercise to improve your high notes. Play the repeated bars many times over, slowly at first.

Keep your hand movements to a minimum. Don't forget to check your intonation.

Exercise 4:

Another chromatic exercise to help improve your low notes. You will need strong little fingers for this and lots of patience. This one is Hard (with a capital H)!

Pieces for Lesson 25

When And Where

Ned Bennett

You should learn both parts. Good intonation is vital to make this piece work.

Watch out for chromatic passages.

Pieces for Lesson 25

CD2 22–23

Spring Song

Mendelssohn

Grazioso

CD2 24–25

Entry Of The Gladiators

Fučík

First practice this famous tune slowly to work out the notes. Don't lose patience…it's well worth the effort!

Moderato

goals:

1. The Blues scale
2. Improvisation

The Blues scale

The Blues is a style of music that originated in the American South during the beginning of the 20th century.

Originally a Blues musician would sing while accompanying himself on guitar but, from the 1920s, the Blues was played on piano, saxophone, trumpet, and most jazz instruments.

Most of the melodic content of the Blues uses the Blues scale, a series of notes that gives the music its special character.

Huddie Ledbetter (Leadbelly)

Exercise 1:

There is a Blues scale for every key. Here is the Blues scale in G.

Exercise 2:

Here is a short melody to illustrate how the notes of the Blues scale can sound.
Notice that you can extend the scale above and below the key notes.

Improvisation

One very essential part of Blues (and jazz) is *improvisation*. This means that the musician makes up the melody as he or she goes along. The Blues scale makes this quite easy, as it will fit with all the different chords that accompany the Blues.

Exercise 3:

Make sure you have practiced the G Blues scale so that you can play it without looking.
Play the following four bars. Can't see any notes? Then you'll have to make something up as you go along, but keep the tempo steady!

Pieces for Lesson 26

CD2
26–27

Holy-Moly Blues

Ned Bennett

Play the notated bars as written. Improvise the blank bars using only the notes of the G Blues scale.
The slashes indicate the beats in these improvised bars. If you can't think of anything to play, either repeat
the notated bar you have just played, or don't play at all...rests are a very important part of all music!

CD2
28–29

Play This Funky Music

Ned Bennett

Funk is a more modern style than Blues, although it shares many characteristics. Don't swing the eighth
notes, and remember to take the *D.C. al Fine* after your improvisation. Sixteen bars may seem like a long time,
but it will be over before you know it.

Exercise 4:

Here is the Blues scale in E, ascending and descending over two octaves.

Make sure you can play it fluently and from memory before attempting the next piece.

Alabama Boogie-Woogie

Ned Bennett

CD2
30

Traditional Blues uses a 12-bar chord sequence to tie the music together.

This piece follows the 12-bar Blues form. Play the "head" (melody), then two choruses of improvisation, then the head once more, remembering to go to the Coda to finish.

Boogie-Woogie was originally a style of Blues played on the piano. The left hand would play a repeated rhythm throughout that gave the music its driving nature.

Medium Swing Tempo

Lesson 27 goals:

1. Eighth-note triplets
2. Minor scales

Eighth-note triplets

Triplets are a set of three notes that occupy the time that would normally be taken up by two notes of the same value. Look at the following comparison.

Each of the three groups contains notes that add up to one quarter note. Eighth-note triplets (a group of three eighth notes with a "3" written above or below) must be played faster than ordinary eighth notes, but not as fast at sixteenth notes.

Exercise 1:

Play this with a slow and steady beat. Putting a slight accent on the notes that coincide with a beat.

Count: 1 2 3 4 1 2 3 4 1 2 3 4 1 2 3 4 1...

Exercise 2: Eighth notes and eighth-note triplets

It is easy to make the mistake of playing triplets as a group of two sixteenth notes followed by an eighth note. Make sure all three notes are exactly the same length. Try this tongued and slurred as indicated.

As outlined in book 1, scale practice will help you to:

• Train your fingers to respond quickly in various keys
• Ensure evenness in the timing of notes
• Develop a consistent tone over the range of the instrument
• Increase control over your breathing
• Improve your listening awareness of note relationships

Exercise 3: Two new minor scales:

G minor

E minor

Pieces for Lesson 27

La donna è mobile from Rigoletto

Verdi

CD2 31

Here's a very happy tune from a very sad opera. Make sure the dotted pairs are exact.

Barry O'Flynn

Irish Folk Song

CD2 32-33

The instruction "with a swing" actually makes this piece easier. Like jazz, many Irish tunes are written down in the way that's easiest to read.

Pieces for Lesson 27

Valse No. 9 (Op. 69, No. 1)

Chopin

Chopin wrote many extremely fast pieces for piano. However, some of his most beautiful music is slow and lyrical. This must be played exactly as written. Although it looks hard, there is a lot of repetition, and remember: *lento* means "slowly," which will help.

goals:

1. Quarter-note triplets
2. Acciaccaturas

Quarter-note triplets

Just as eighth-note triplets occupy the space of two regular eighth notes, a quarter-note triplet fits into the space of two ordinary quarter notes.

Count: **1   2   3   4   1   2   3   4**

You can see the difficulty here is that while the first note of each group of triplets falls on a beat, the second and third fall on either side of the next beat.

Exercise 1:

Play both of the following. What do you notice?

Andante

Allegro

Exercise 2:

The accents are there to help you because they always coincide with beats 1 and 3.
Be careful not to play quarter-note triplets as an eighth note–quarter note–eighth note rhythm.

Acciaccatura

This is a very long word for an extremely short note. An acciaccatura (pronounced atch-akka-tour-a) may be written as a small eighth note or a sixteenth note with a slash through the tail, but should last no time at all and be slurred to the main note. Whether the acciaccatura comes *just before* the beat or right on it is a topic of hot debate in classical circles: let your sense of style and phrasing be your guide!

Exercise 3:

Pieces for Lesson 28

CD2
36-37

Triplet Trouble Blues

Ned Bennett

Take this slowly, but still play the acciaccaturas quickly and on the beat, not before.

CD2
38

To The Spring

Edvard Grieg

Listen to the quarter note count-in very carefully. The accompaniment consists of quarter-note triplets, which may make it difficult for you to find the pulse!

Pieces for Lesson 28

Moment Musical

Schubert

No triplets to worry about here. However, there are plenty of acciaccaturas.

Lesson 29

goals:

1. **Improving your tone**
2. **Breath control**
3. **More dynamics**

Improving your tone

There must have been something about the saxophone that made you want to learn to play one. Although the instrument *looks* cool, it has a unique sound that can make the hair on the back of your neck stand on end.

Your tone should be clear, with very little breath noise or hiss. Push enough air through the saxophone to achieve a moderately loud and bright tone that doesn't "wobble." If you are finding this hard, check that your reed is correctly positioned and undamaged.

Try to record yourself playing one of your favorite pieces from this book. You don't have to hire a recording studio: most computers can record sound, and schools and colleges often have a good recording device. Listen to the recording. How do you sound compared to your teacher or your favorite sax player on CD?

A great tone takes years to develop. It is not just knowing what to do, it is also building up muscles (or *chops* as jazz musicians say), just like an athlete would to compete at the highest level.

The following *chops* exercises could be thought of as your saxophone gym routine.
The more you play these exercises, the better you will sound.
You won't need your brain once you are familiar with the exercises, so walk about, or look out the window while playing them.

Try to spend five to ten minutes, three times a week, on this routine.

Chops exercise 1:

Breathe in slowly and deeply.
Play the first note for a count of 4. Slur to the lower note and hold it on for the rest of your breath.
Keep pushing out air, until you really have none left in your lungs.
Relax, breathe in slowly and play the next pair. (In the 2nd pair, play the G♯ as a G with the low C♯ key held down.)

This exercise is to:

- Build muscles so you can keep your throat open at all times when playing
- Enlarge your lung capacity and control your airflow using your diaphragm
- Build muscles in both little fingers

Chops exercise 2:

Breathe as you did for Chops exercise 1, but only one note per breath here. Do not change the fingering for any of the notes. The first note is played with an open throat. To get the second note, increase the speed of the air by pushing a little more with your diaphragm and tighten your bottom lip slightly without closing your jaw. The third note requires an even firmer bottom lip.

Try not to tighten your embouchure to get these higher notes otherwise the tone will be thin. If you can, concentrate on moving your jaws slightly further apart by dropping your chin.

Practice this in front of a mirror. Check that your embouchure appears "round" and not "wide."

This exercise is to:

- Build muscles so you can keep your throat open at all times when playing
- Improve your diaphragm control
- Enlarge your mouth cavity to produce a fuller and sweeter tone
- Build muscle strength in your bottom lip

Remember—keep the fingering for low C throughout.

Dynamic Extremes

Up till now you have played music with dynamics ranging anywhere from quiet to loud (p to f).
As your strength and control increases, you could be asked to play very quiet (*pianissimo*) pp, or very loud (*fortissimo*) ff.

Chops exercise 3:

Breathe in slowly and deeply. Play each note for as long as possible, moving very slowly and perfectly smoothly through the dynamics as indicated. Ensure that all notes are in tune.

This exercise is to:

- Increase your diaphragm control
- Improve your intonation
- Improve your tone by building muscles through long notes

Adagietto from Symphony No. 5

Mahler

This should be slow, and very expressive—it ranks among the most passionate music ever written.

1. Practice routine
2. Trills

Practice routine

There is one basic fact that applies to playing every musical instrument: **the more you practice, the quicker you will improve**. Some people enjoy practicing and others don't. However, a fixed daily routine is essential to make the best of your time.

- Try to practice at the same time every day
- Be focused: keep your mind entirely on your practicing
- Remember your goals for the week (new pieces, scales, etc.)

- Spend a good amount of time on technical work; don't just play your favorite pieces
- Don't be impatient: remember that you will be a better player for having practiced

Use the following table to log your practice for this week.
Be honest...this is to help you work out how to improve at a quicker pace.

Day	Long note warm-ups	Chops _or_ Intonation Exercise		Scales	Pieces	Total minutes
		Chops	**Intonation**			

Trills

Although usually found in music from the Baroque era (1600-1750) and the Classical era (1750-1820), trills are a very important form of ornamentation in many styles of music. The written note is rapidly alternated with the note above:

Not exact sixteenth notes, just as fast as possible.

For music written before 1750, begin the trill on the upper note.

Pieces for Lesson 30

Gavotte from Suite No. 3

J. S. Bach (1685-1750)

Look at Bach's dates: on which notes do the trills begin?

* Use the side B♭ fingering here. Keep the side key pressed as you alternate with the C.

Pieces for Lesson 30

Flor, Bianca Flor

Mexican Folk Song

This is from the 19th century. Keep the rhythm straight, although there is room for expressive playing.
Your trills should be coordinated if possible.

1. Rubato
2. Solo playing

Rubato

Sometimes, subtly altering the tempo during a piece of music can be very expressive.
Soloists often use a kind of hesitation, or slowing down, to achieve a dramatic effect.
This is known as *rubato* (Italian for "robbed") and is especially effective when used sparingly.

Originally rubato passages "borrowed" time by slowing down, and then caught up with the accompaniment by speeding up later in the phrase. Nowadays playing rubato simply means being flexible with the tempo of the performance to create expression.

A good soloist will know the music by heart. This gives the performer confidence and helps the music to flow much more convincingly.

Solo playing

In most music auditions, an unaccompanied piece tests your ability to play *solo*. You may also be asked to perform in a concert, or you may want to play for your friends and family.

A guide for solo playing

• If the piece has a lively rhythm, it is essential that you keep the beat steady. Music is a language, and if people can tap their toes to what you are playing, you are communicating with them.

• Never perform a piece so fast that you have to slow down for the tricky passages. Practice everything at one tempo and gradually speed up the whole piece.

• If the piece is dreamier in nature, then allow yourself some rubato. Enjoy the feeling of power that you can control your audience. Make them wait for expressive moments, or increase their excitement by pushing the tempo a little faster.

• Whatever the piece, always think before you play. Try to hear the beginning of the piece in your head... breathe...breathe again... then play.

Solo Pieces for Lesson 31

Sailor's Hornpipe
English Folk Dance

Traditionally this piece begins very slowly and gradually builds up tempo to a fast, rousing conclusion.
However, make sure you can play it all perfectly at a moderate tempo before you try anything fancy.

Sometimes I Feel Like A Motherless Child
Spiritual

Here's an opportunity for rubato. Learn the piece keeping to a strict, slow tempo. Then think how you might
make it more expressive by changing this at times.

Solo Pieces for Lesson 31

100% Humidity

Ned Bennett

Swing this piece which uses the E Blues scale. Keep the tempo steady (no rubato), and repeat the improvisation section as many times as you like. You must always relate the notes to the beat which should remain implied by what you play. Take the ideas for your improvisation from the written music if you wish.

Medium Shuffle

(E Blues scale)

goals:

1. Simple time, compound time, and unusual time signatures
2. More scales

Time signatures

In *simple* time signatures the beat can be divided into two. It means that the music flows predictably and this is why these signatures are the most commonly found:

In *compound* time signatures the beat divides into three. The music still flows well.

All the pieces that you have played so far in this book use a time signature from the illustrations above. However, many pieces deliberately use a less-flowing time signature:

Exercise 1:

Clap the following examples, emphasizing the notes on which accents have been placed.

By the way, the time signature may change at any point in a piece! Have a look at the *Bulgarian Dance* later in this lesson to see an example of this.

Lesson 32

Exercise 2: New scales and arpeggios

E♭ major

Scale:

Arpeggio:

F♯ minor

Scale:

Arpeggio:

Play these according to the time signatures and accents (although normally you should play them with equal weighting for each note).

Pieces for Lesson 32

CD2
46–47

Bulgarian Dance

Energetically

Pieces for Lesson 32

Ut tuo propitiatus

11th Century Organum

At first this piece may sound odd, perhaps rather modern and experimental, even though it was written almost a thousand years ago.

Try to find a church or large hall with lots of reverberation in which to play it. Originally this would have been sung by monks. However, the sound of two saxophones can be equally as haunting.

Don't play this fast, and stick to a strict tempo until the very end.

Lesson 33 goals:

1. **Dexterity**
2. **Increasing speed**

Dexterity

You may have listened to a piece of music that is so fast you can hardly hear the individual notes. When played well, this can sound impressive and exciting. However, it takes a long time and endless patience to develop the skill needed to play very quickly.

Exercise 1:

Practice these exercises regularly, instead of (or in addition to) your intonation and chops exercises.

This exercise uses patterns of the first three notes of every major scale. Make sure you spend more time with the patterns you can't play very well in order to play the whole exercise at a reasonable tempo, both slurred and tongued (which is hard!).

The first key has been written out in full. Play the rest in the same manner.

Exercise 2:

This one is chromatic and happens to work down through the keys, but you could equally work up.

Your little fingers (and side keys) will get a real workout here.

100

Pieces for Lesson 33

Caprice No. 24 (theme)

Paganini

Presto means fast. This piece was originally written for violin, but it has been arranged for piano, cello, and jazz band as well as saxophone.

The Irish Washer Woman

Irish 18th Century

Coordination between your tongue and fingers is essential for this piece.

Pieces for Lesson 33

Czardas

Monti

Play the first (slow) section with just a little rubato. The second section needs to be very fast.

As with all fast music, practice it slowly but in tempo otherwise you will never learn the correct timing.

goals:

1. Endurance
2. Sensitivity

Playing for any length of time puts a strain on your embouchure muscles. Think of running an 800 meter race. The first lap is usually okay, but you will feel the pain in your legs during the second lap. This is because when you tighten your muscles, blood cannot flow through them. Your embouchure muscles go through the same process in a long piece.

To avoid this pain, ensure you release all tension in your bottom lip every time you breathe. Even relaxing for a fraction of a second can allow the blood to flow with its precious oxygen.

Don't forget to be sensitive to the other musicians. In this piece you will sometimes have an interesting melody, but sometimes you will be accompanying other players. Adjust your dynamic level (volume) to reflect this during this 16th century masterpiece.

Alla riva del Tebro (madrigal)
Palestrina

Although the notes in this quartet seem easy, playing it will be hard. Keep your bottom lip relaxed, and make sure you count like crazy. If you get lost you will find it almost impossible to find your place again.

Concert Performance

Having worked through books 1 and 2 of *A New Tune A Day*, you should be ready to perform as part of a concert, whether for friends and family, at school, or for an audience you've never met.

Give yourself the best chance of success with these golden rules.

1. Know your music.

You must be able to play all your pieces, perfectly and without thinking. Musicians play much better if they have memorized the music.

2. Look the part.

Dress professionally, and present yourself as you would for meeting someone very important. This will help you to feel confident when you play.

3. Breathe slowly and deeply before you play.

This will help overcome nerves and oxygenate your brain, helping you to concentrate. It also lets you pause to think about the piece.

4. Bow slowly to the audience when they clap.

This is good manners, as if to say "thank you for listening to me."

Pieces for Lesson 35

The following pieces are all great for a performance. Even if you are playing them just for practice or fun, imagine you are giving a live performance and play with all the expression, technique, and accuracy you can.

Wedding Dance

Kazakhstan

Here is a fiddly melody with many complications, but rewarding to play if you practice it carefully.

Energetic

F and C ped. accomp.

Pieces for Lesson 35

Waltz from Die Fledermaus

Strauss

This is a fine, flowing waltz that needs lots of energy to perform.

This piece is always performed as part of the New Year's Day concert in Vienna, Austria.

Oh, Won't You Sit Down

Spiritual

This piece has been arranged in a jazz style. Play swing eighth notes, and instead of the written notes, play a G Blues scale improvisation in the section marked *solo ad lib* if you prefer.

Pieces for Lesson 35

Hungarian Dance No. 5

Brahms

Finally, an exciting romp to finish the book. Watch out for the tempo changes towards the end, and make sure your fingers know the notes by themselves.

CD 1: backing tracks

How to use the CD

The tuning note on track 1 is concert A, which sounds the same as F♯ on the alto saxophone. After track 2, which gives an idea of how the alto saxophone can sound, the backing tracks are listed in the order in which they appear in the book. Look for the symbol in the book for the relevant backing track. Where both parts of a duet are included on the CD, the top part is in one channel, and the bottom part is in the other channel.

CD 2: backing tracks